Sunshine

Valentine's Day Coloring Book

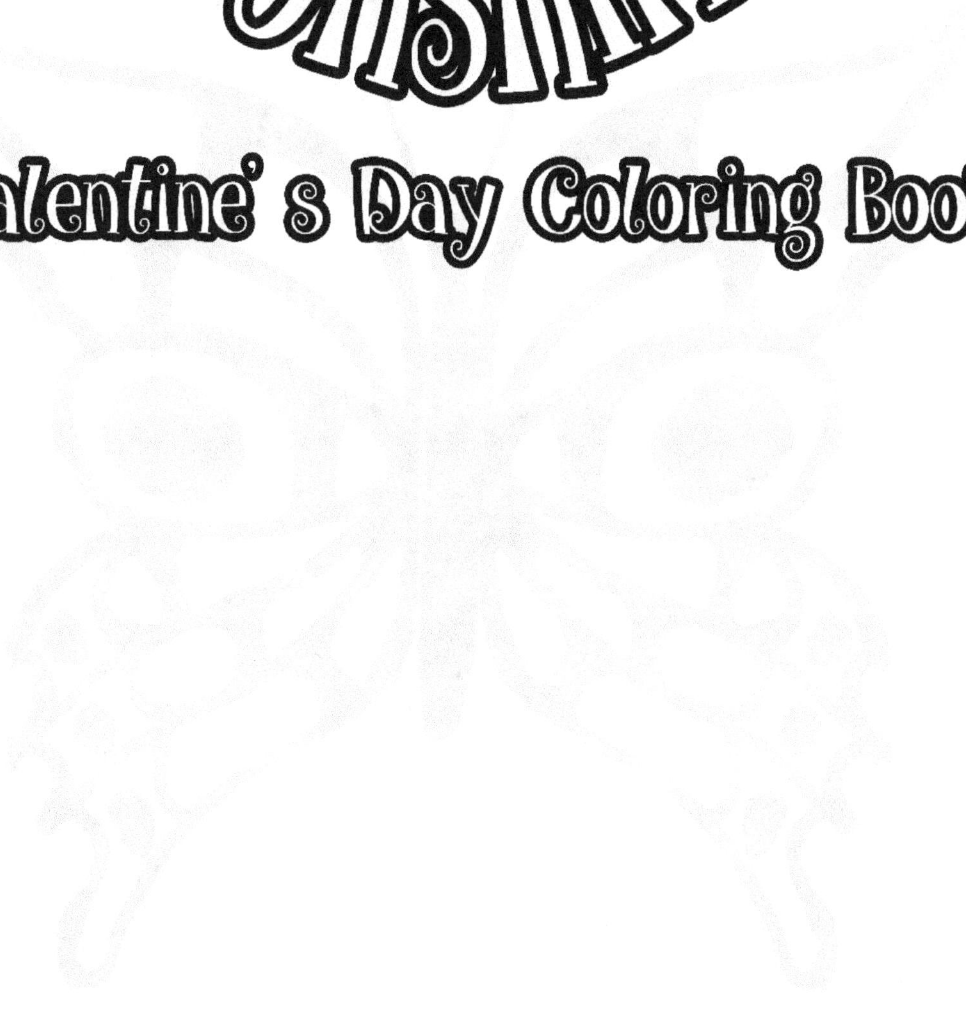

Ayn Eliot

Happy Coloring

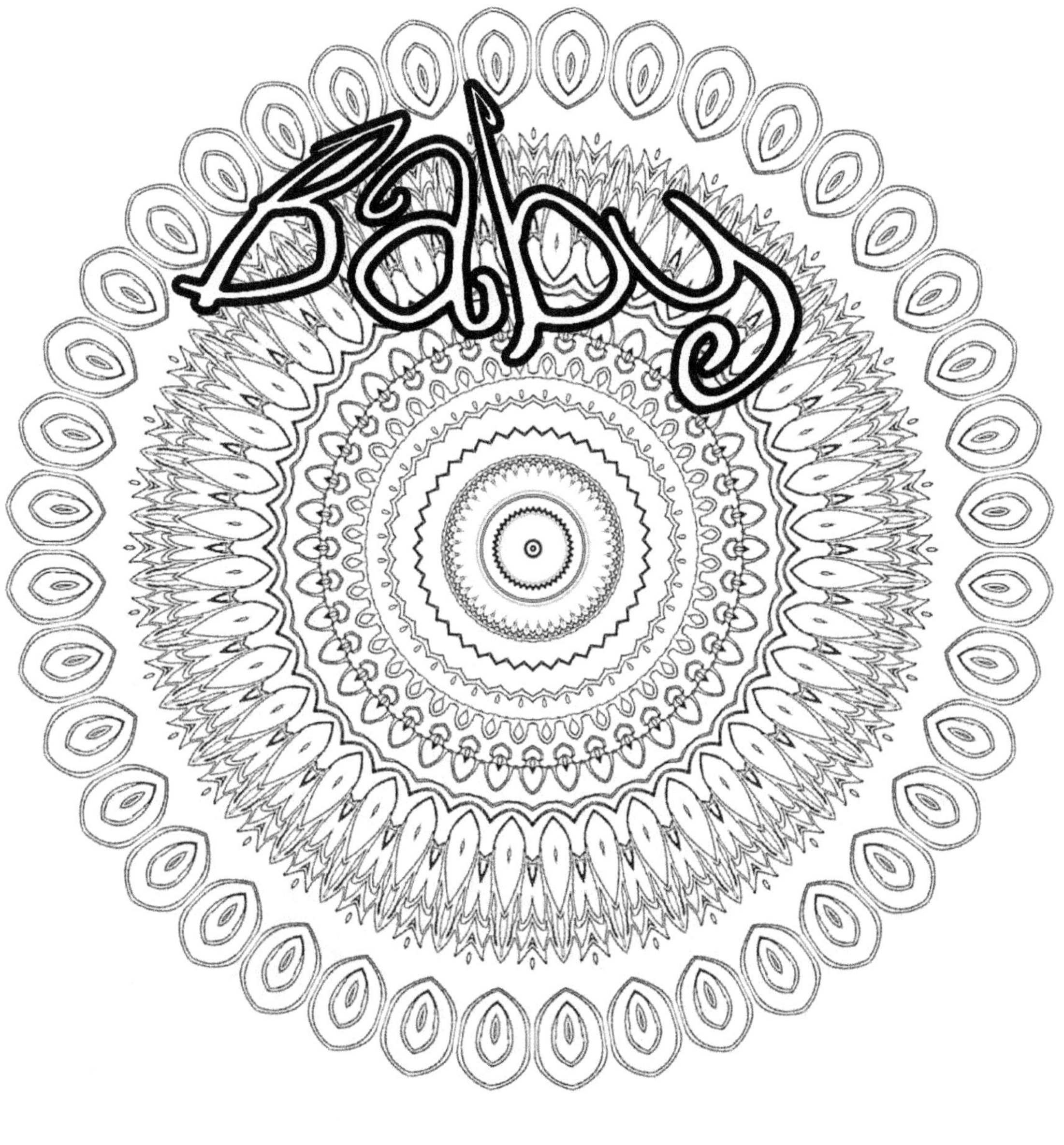
Baby

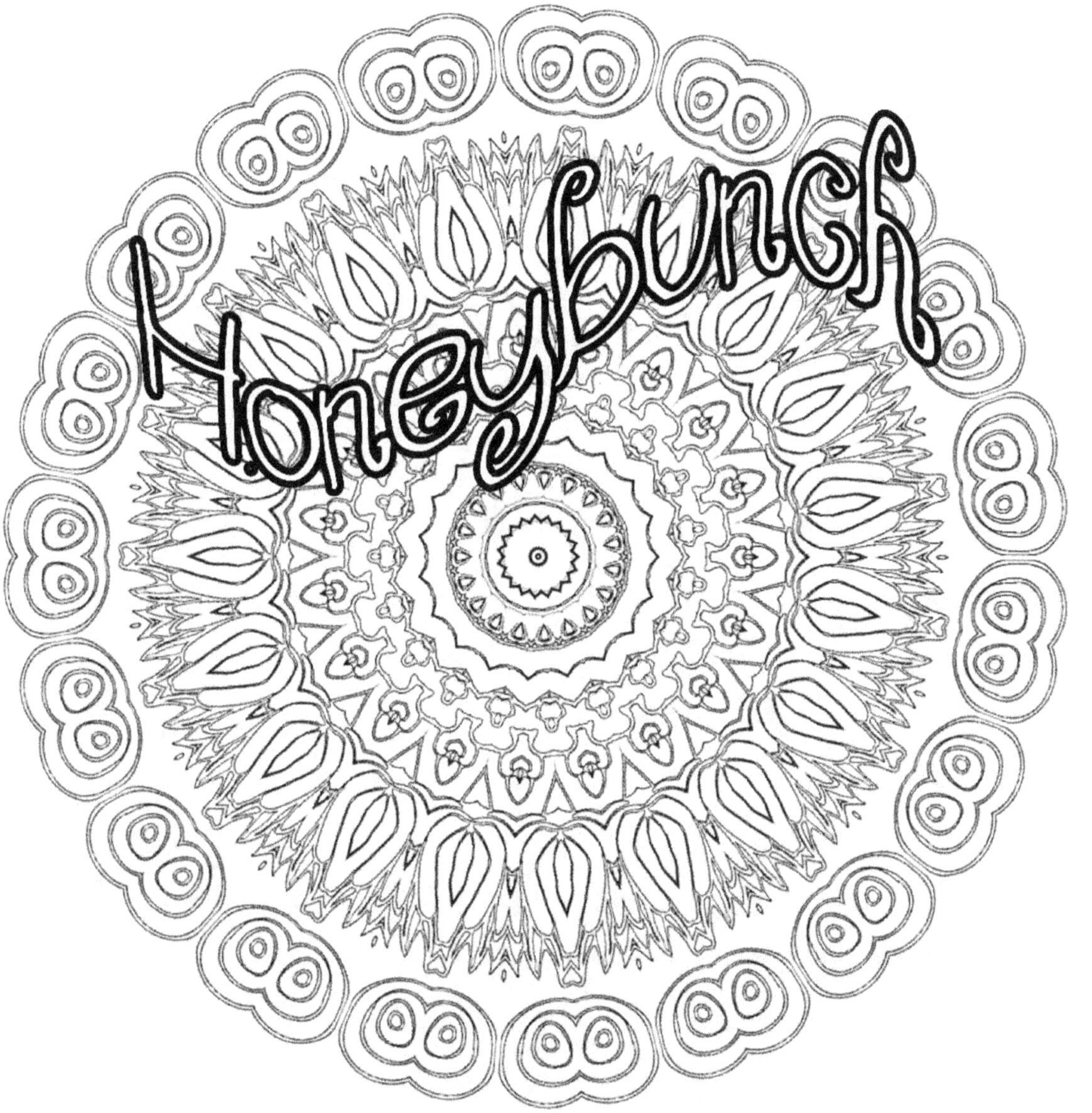
Honeybunch

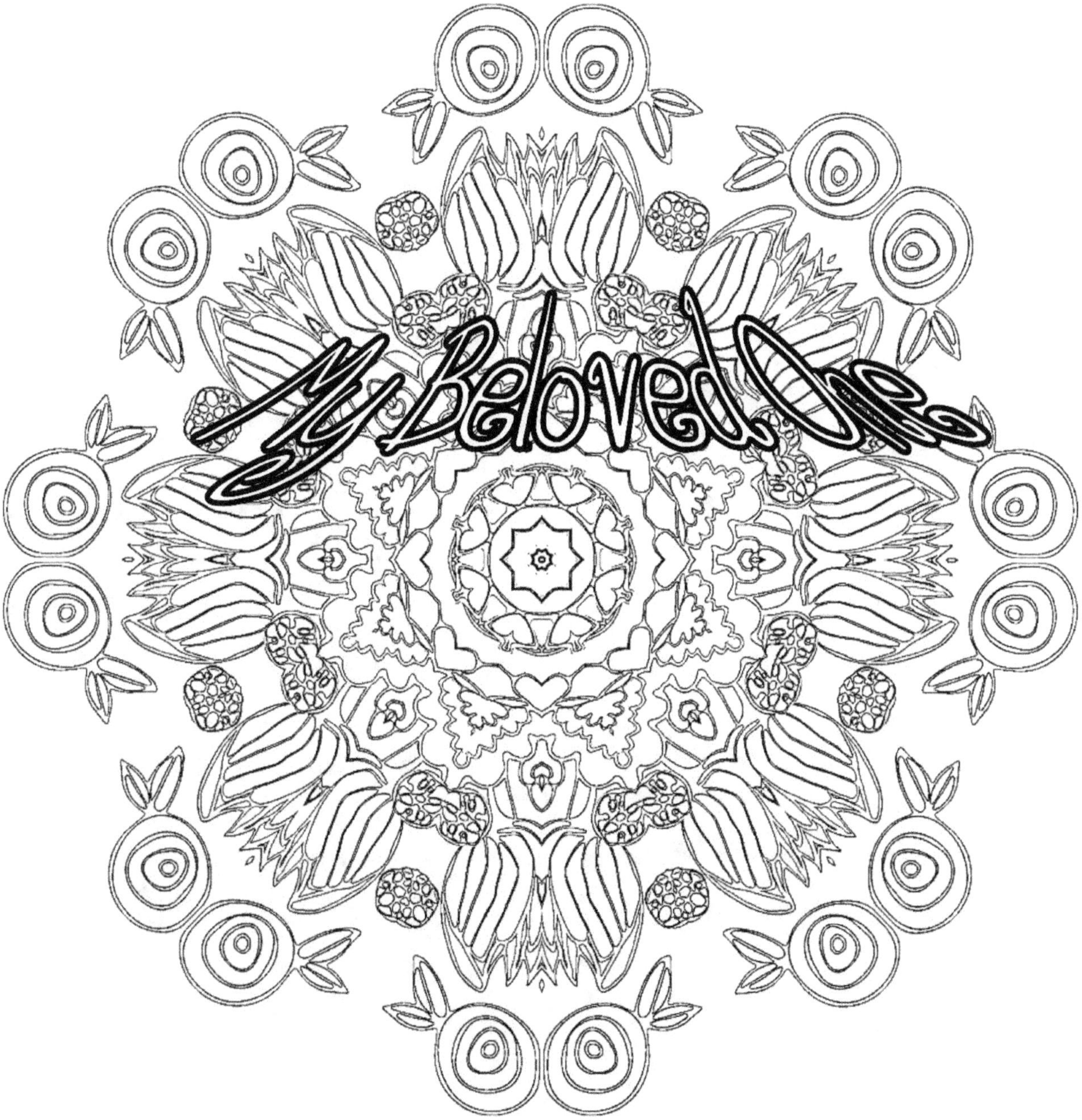
My Beloved One

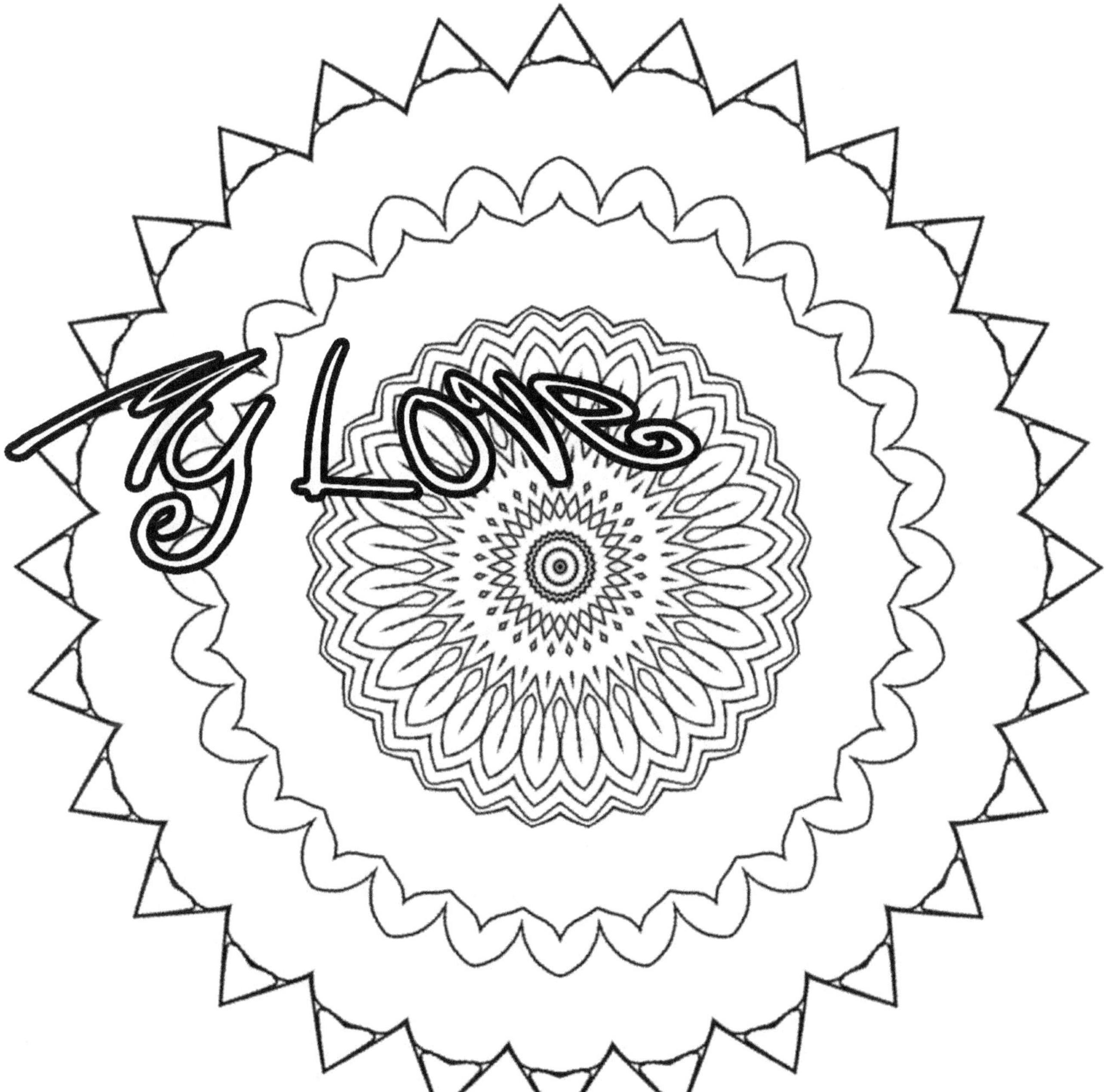
My Love

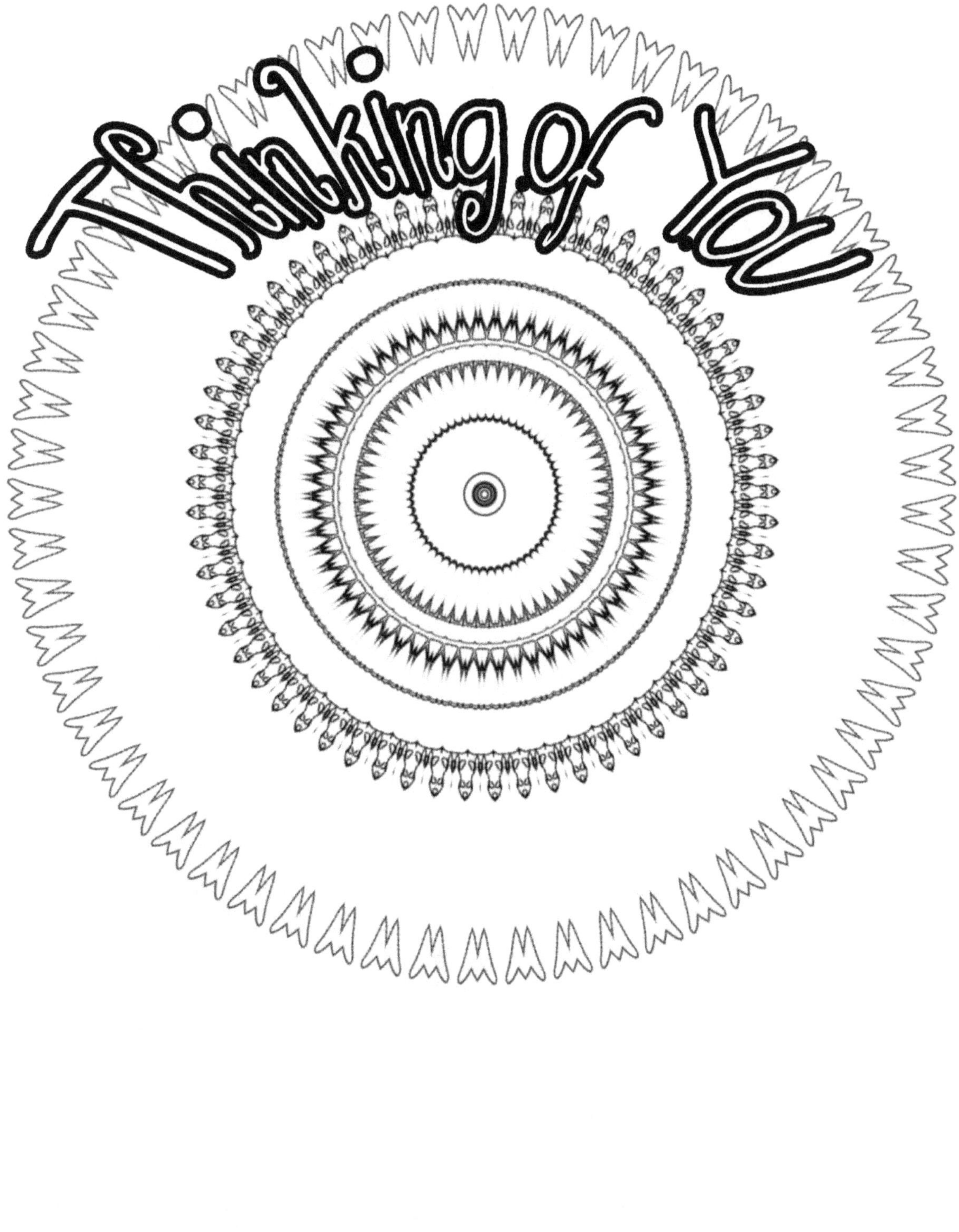
Thinking of You

Dreaming of You

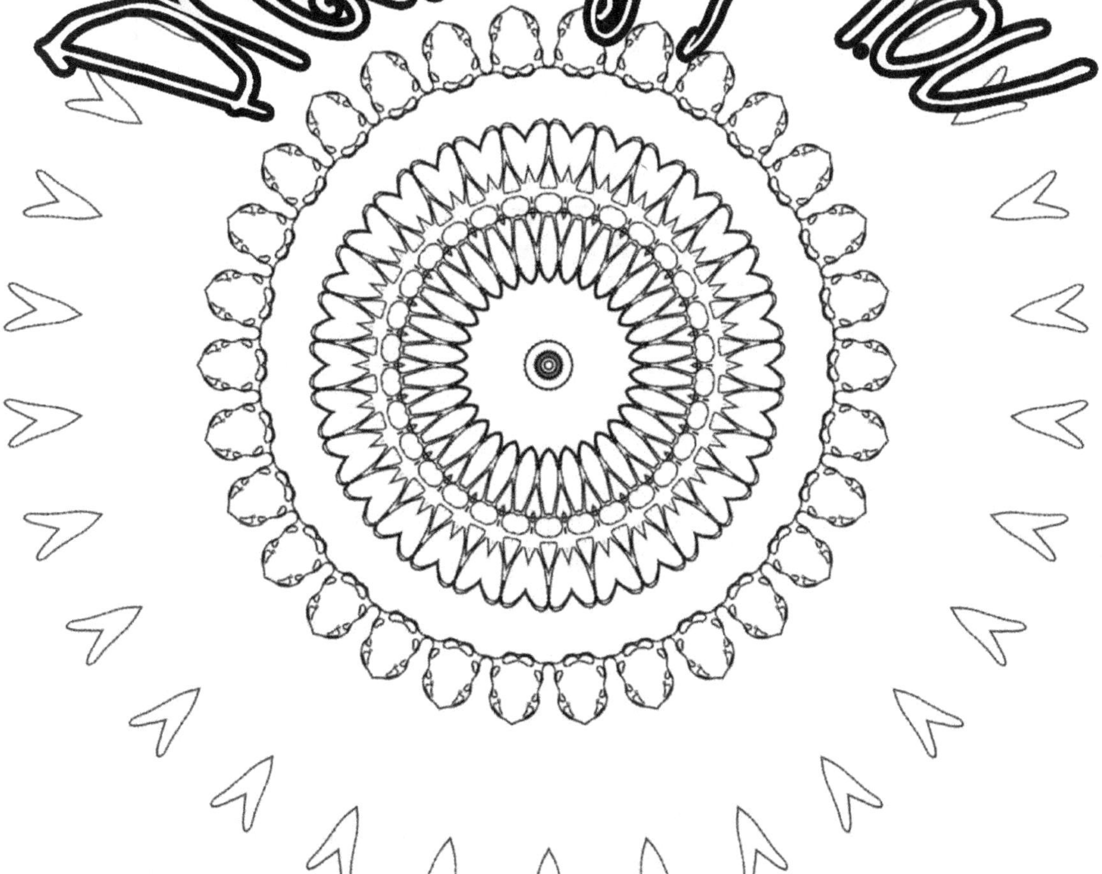

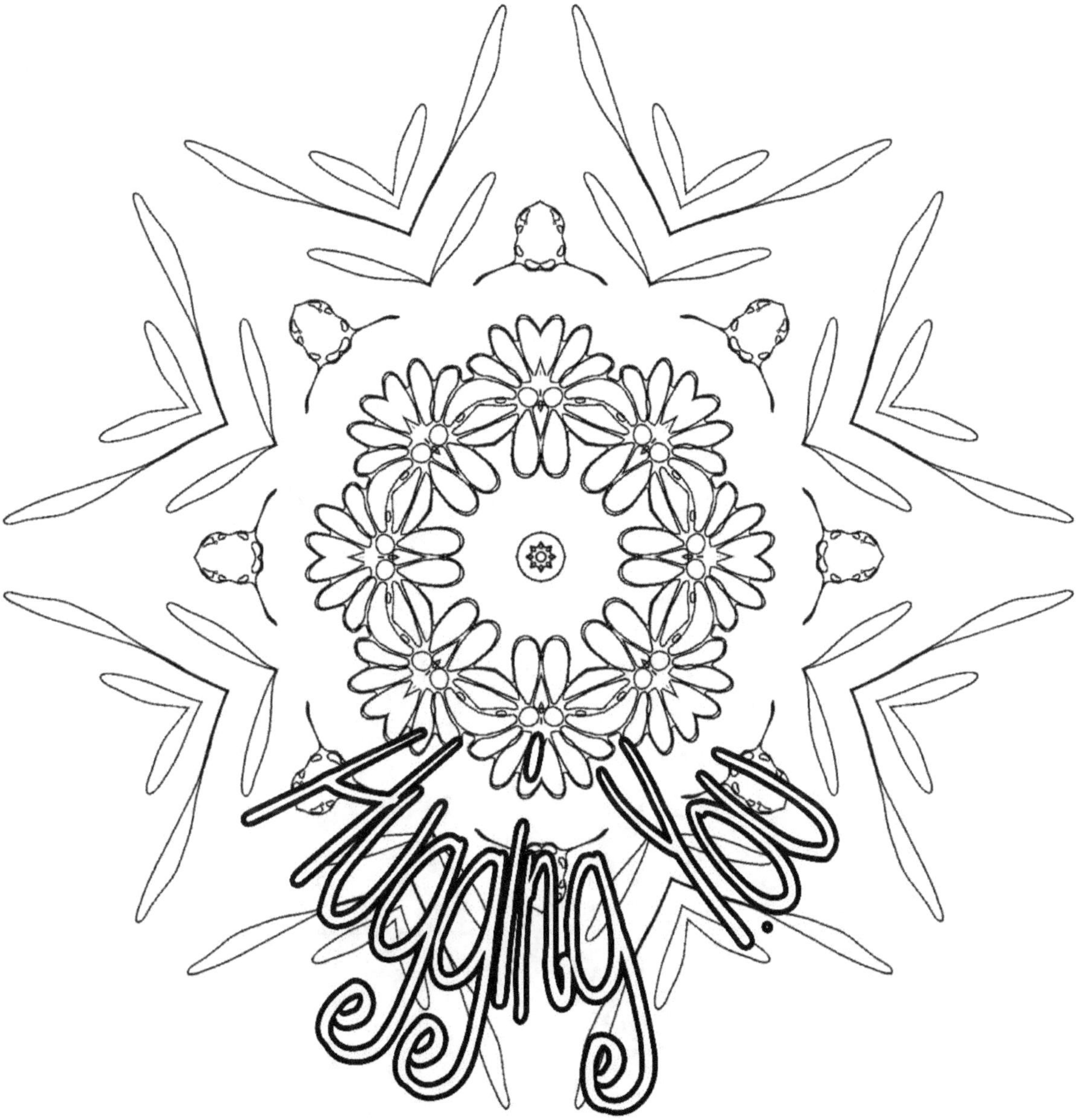
Hugging You.

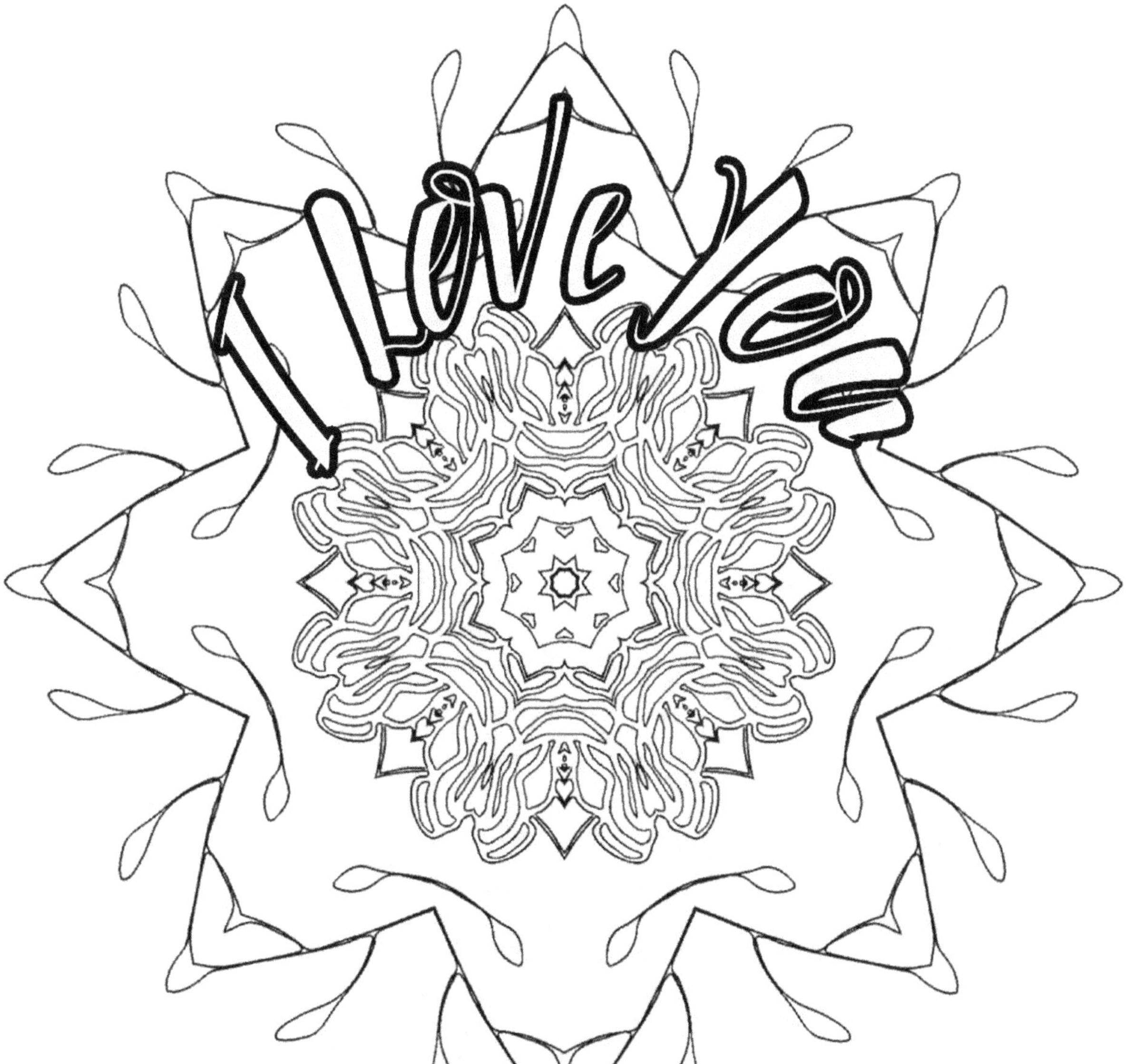
I Love You

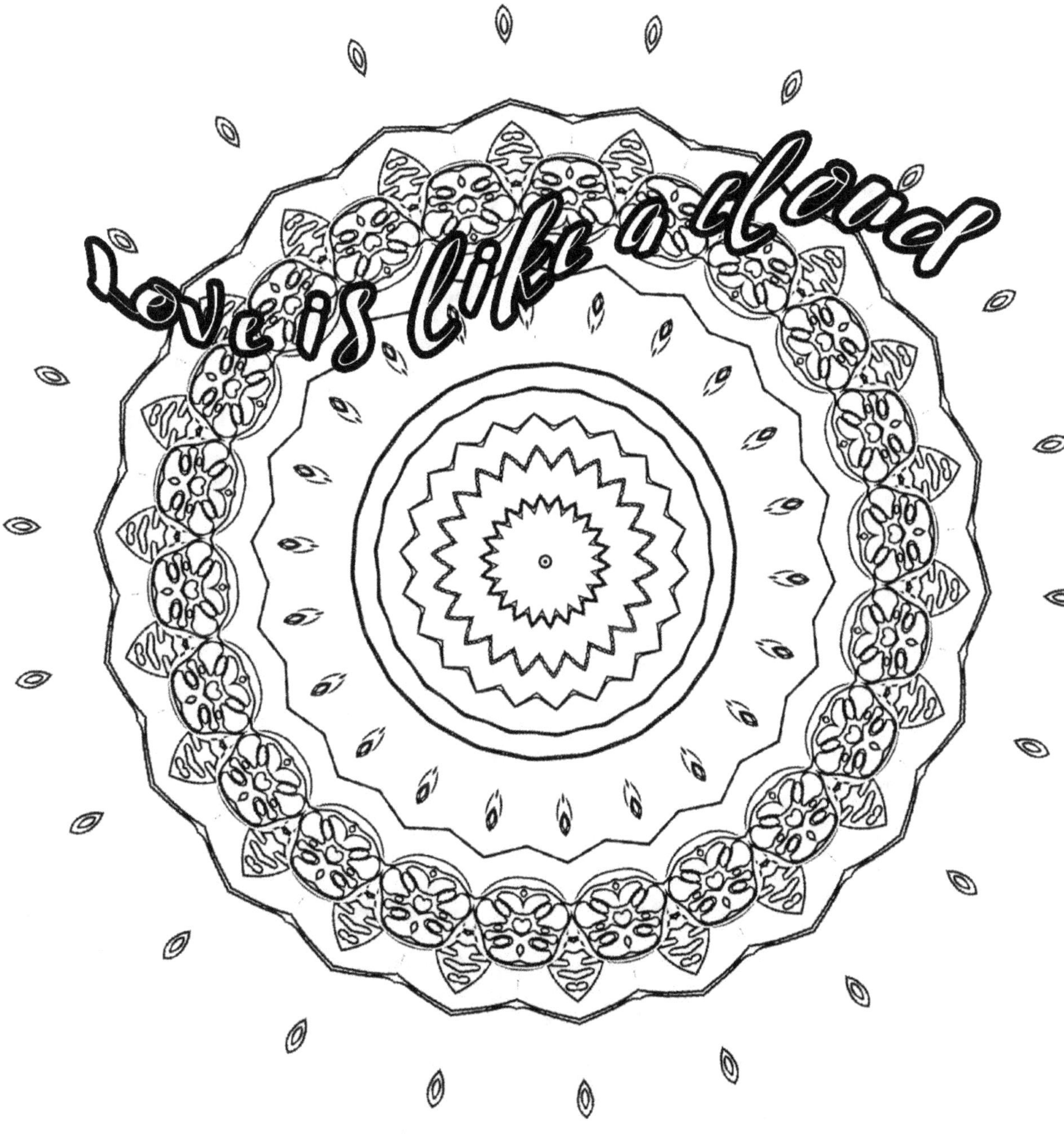
Love is like a cloud

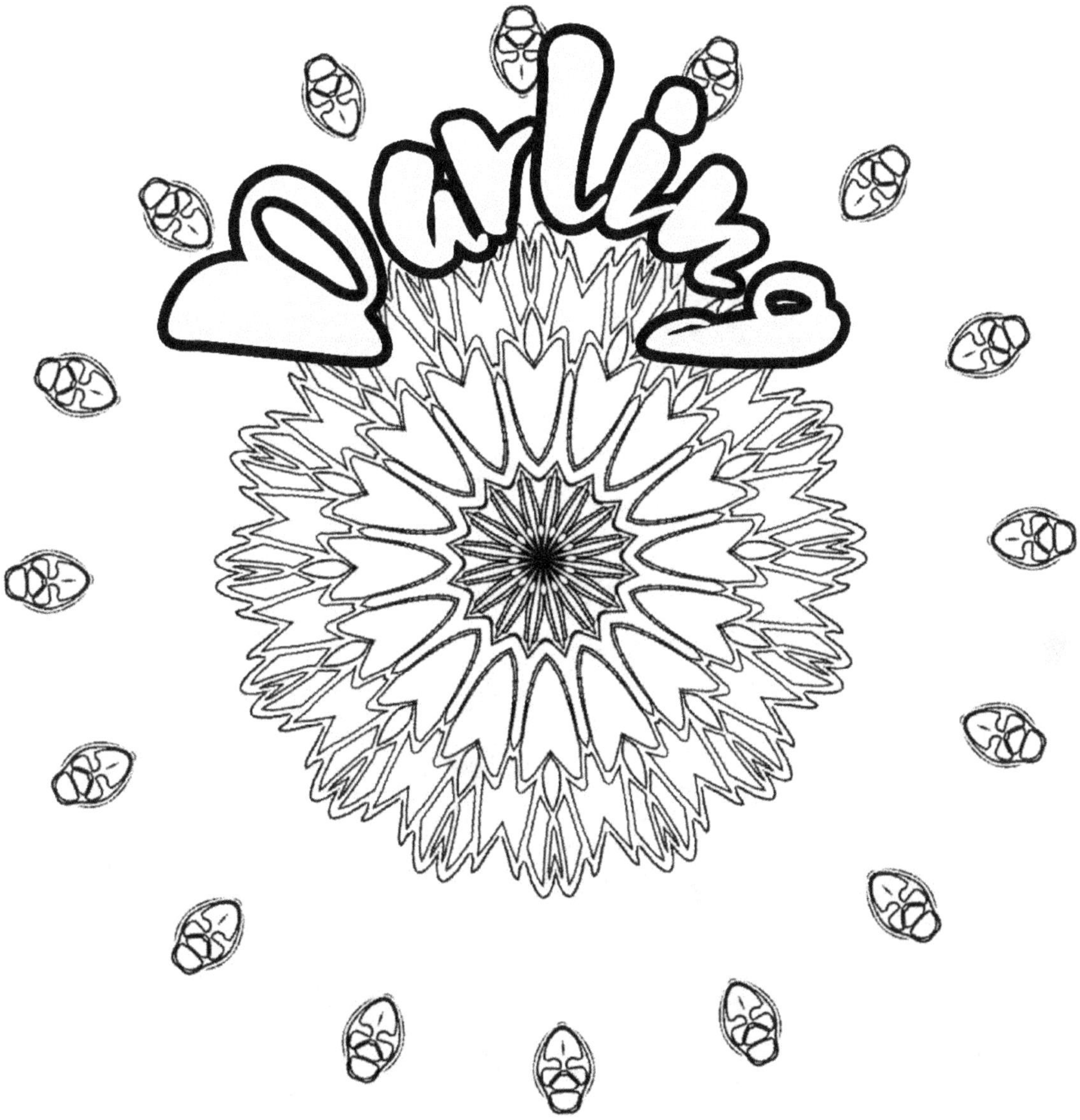
Darling

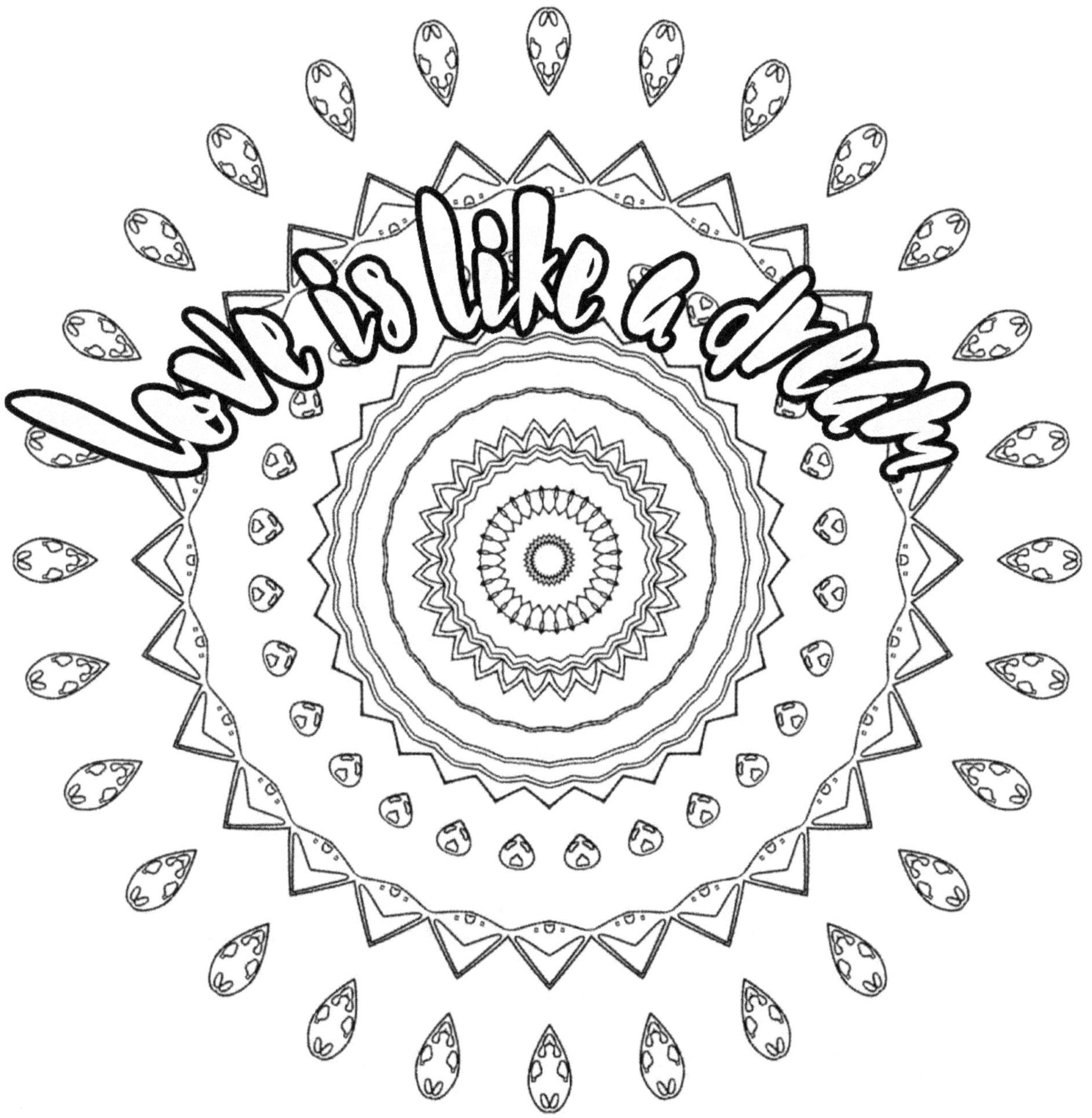
love is like a dream

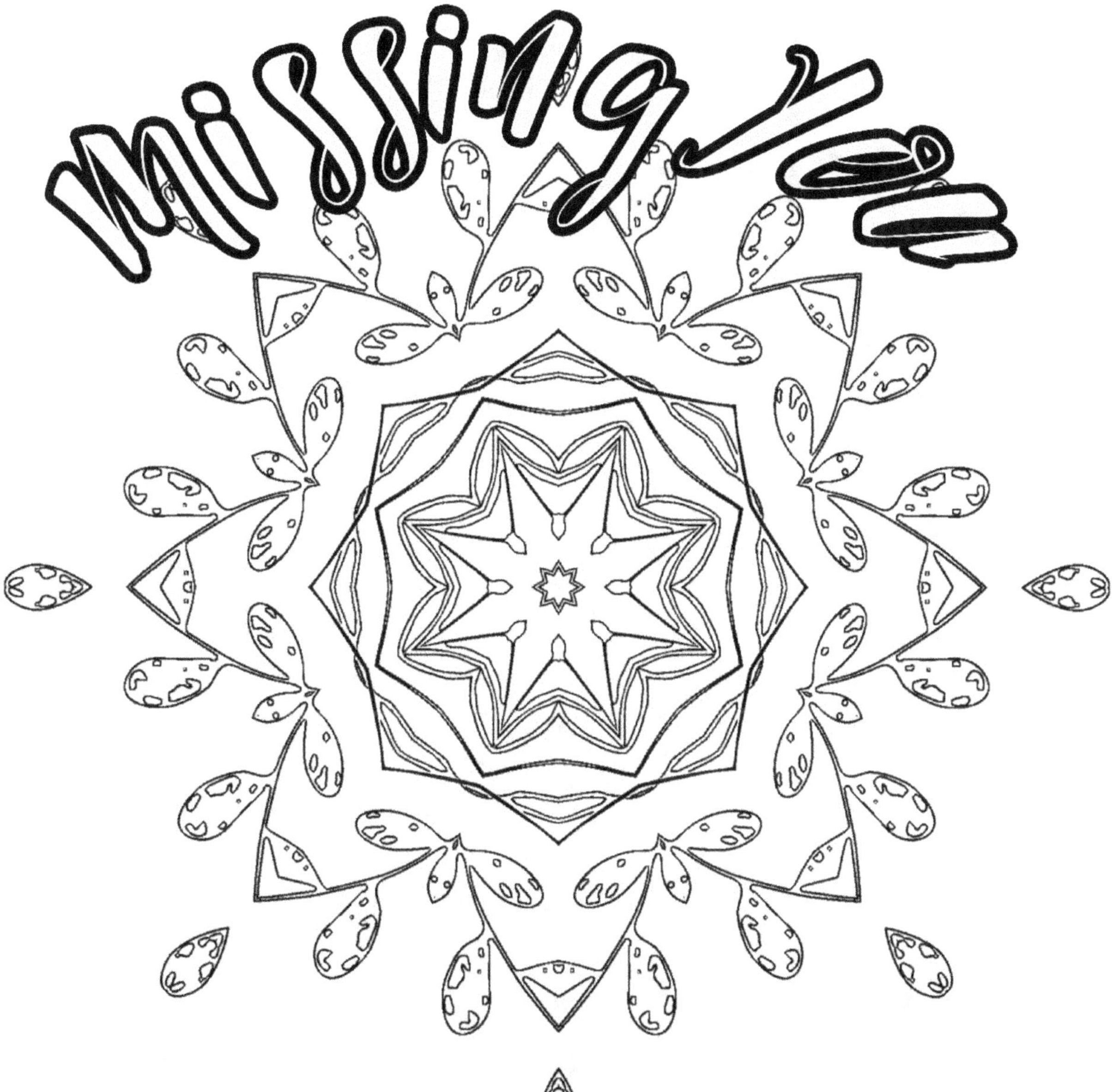
Missing You

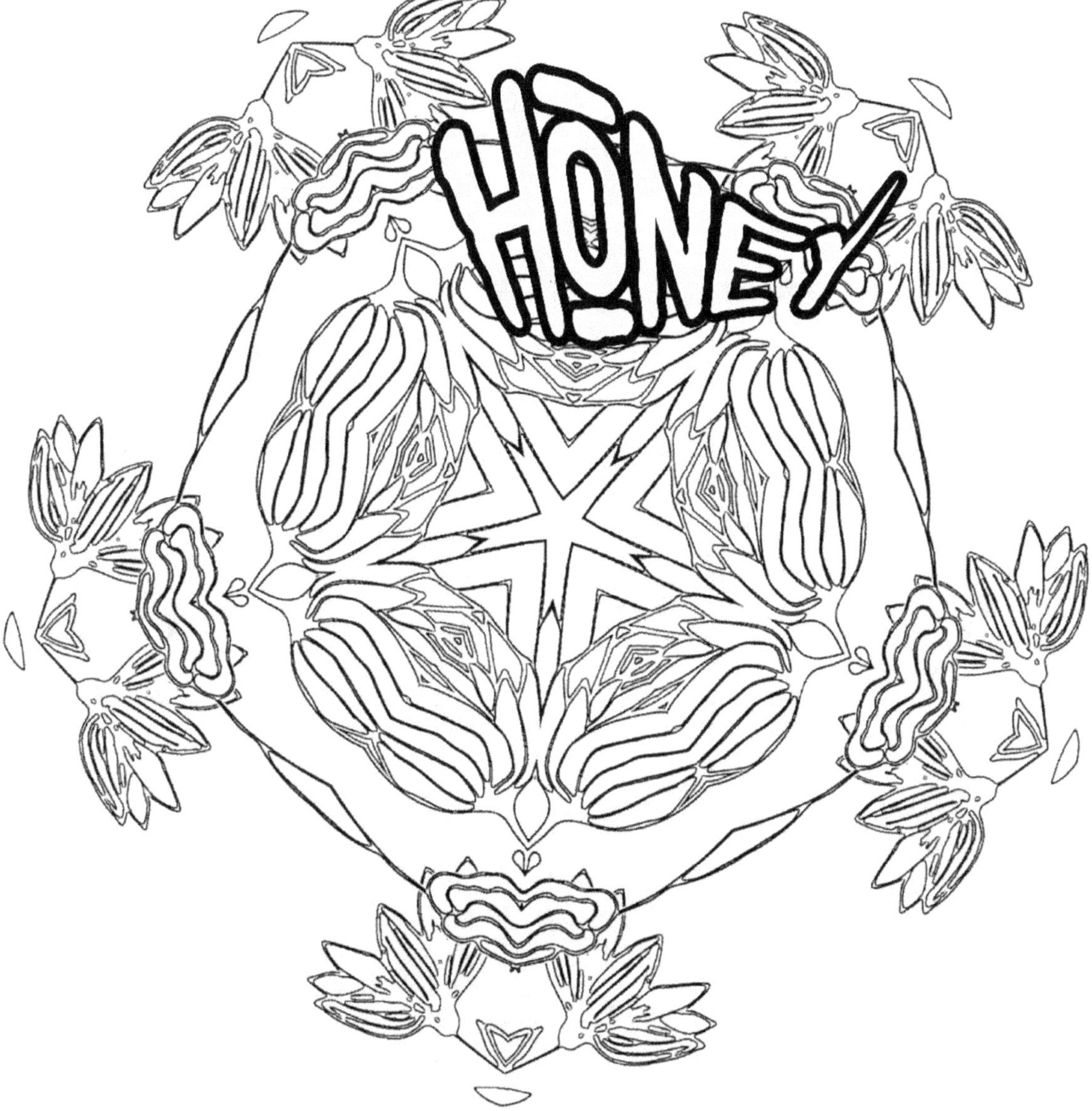
HONEY

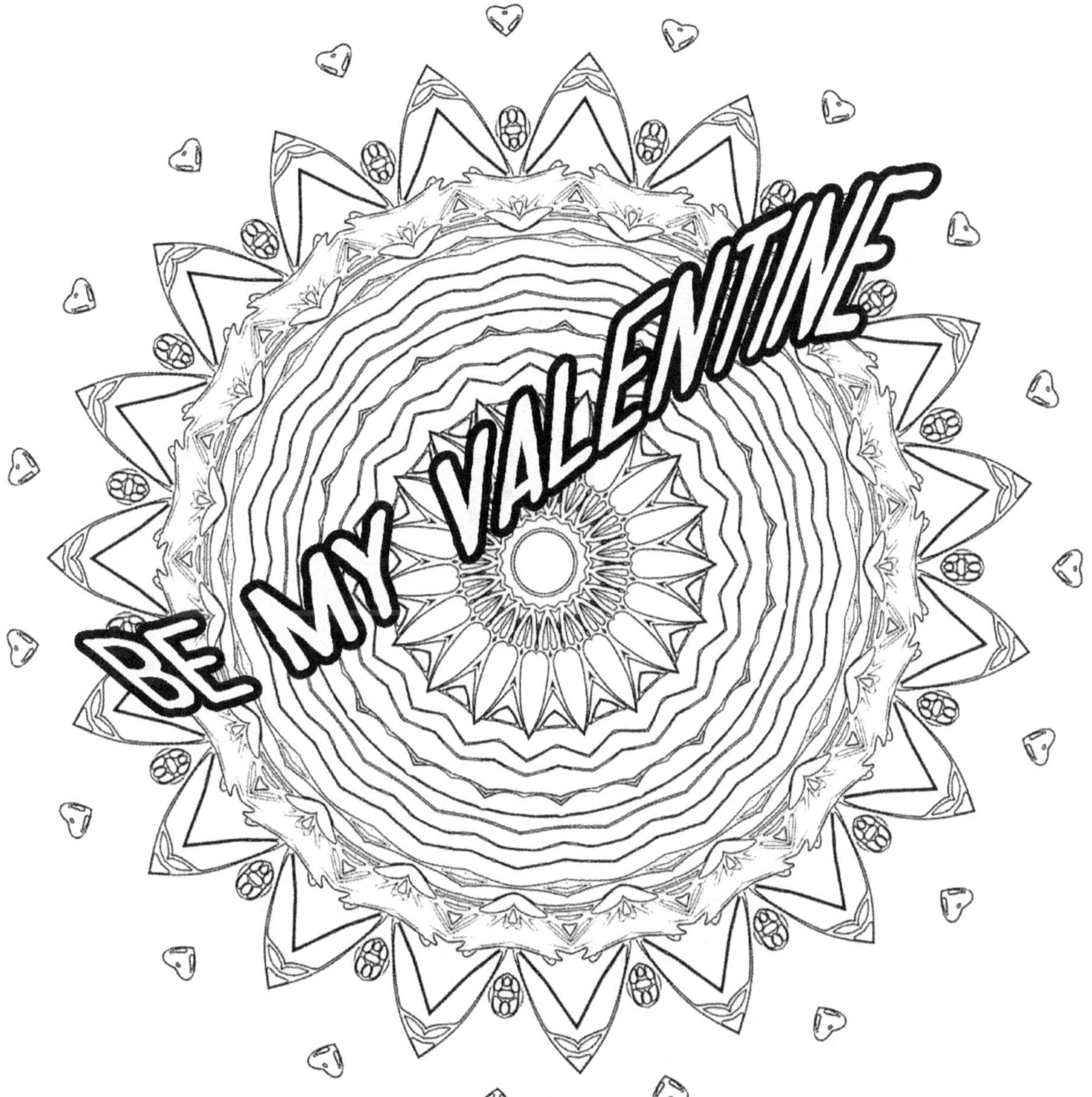
BE MY VALENTINE

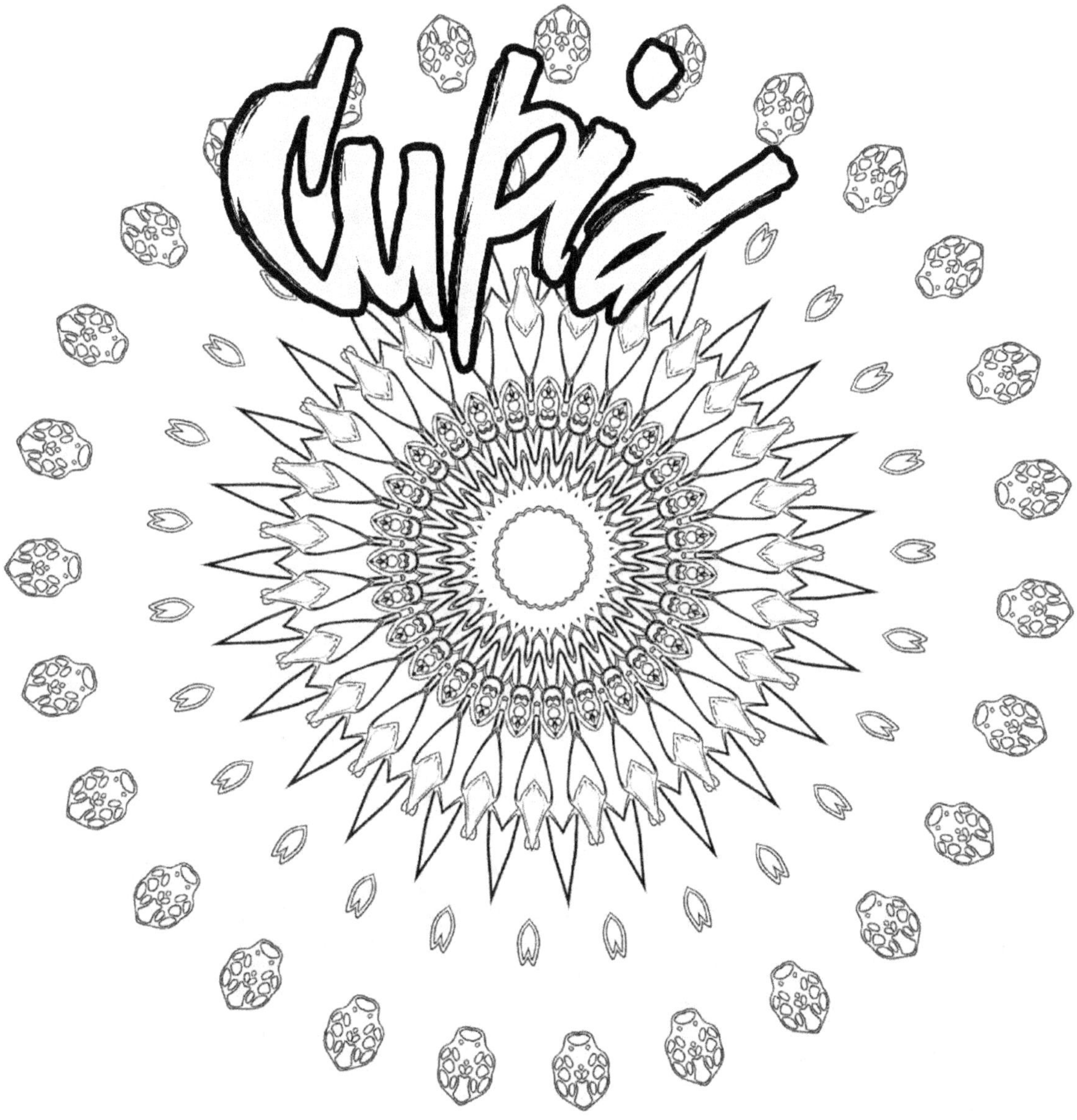
Cupid

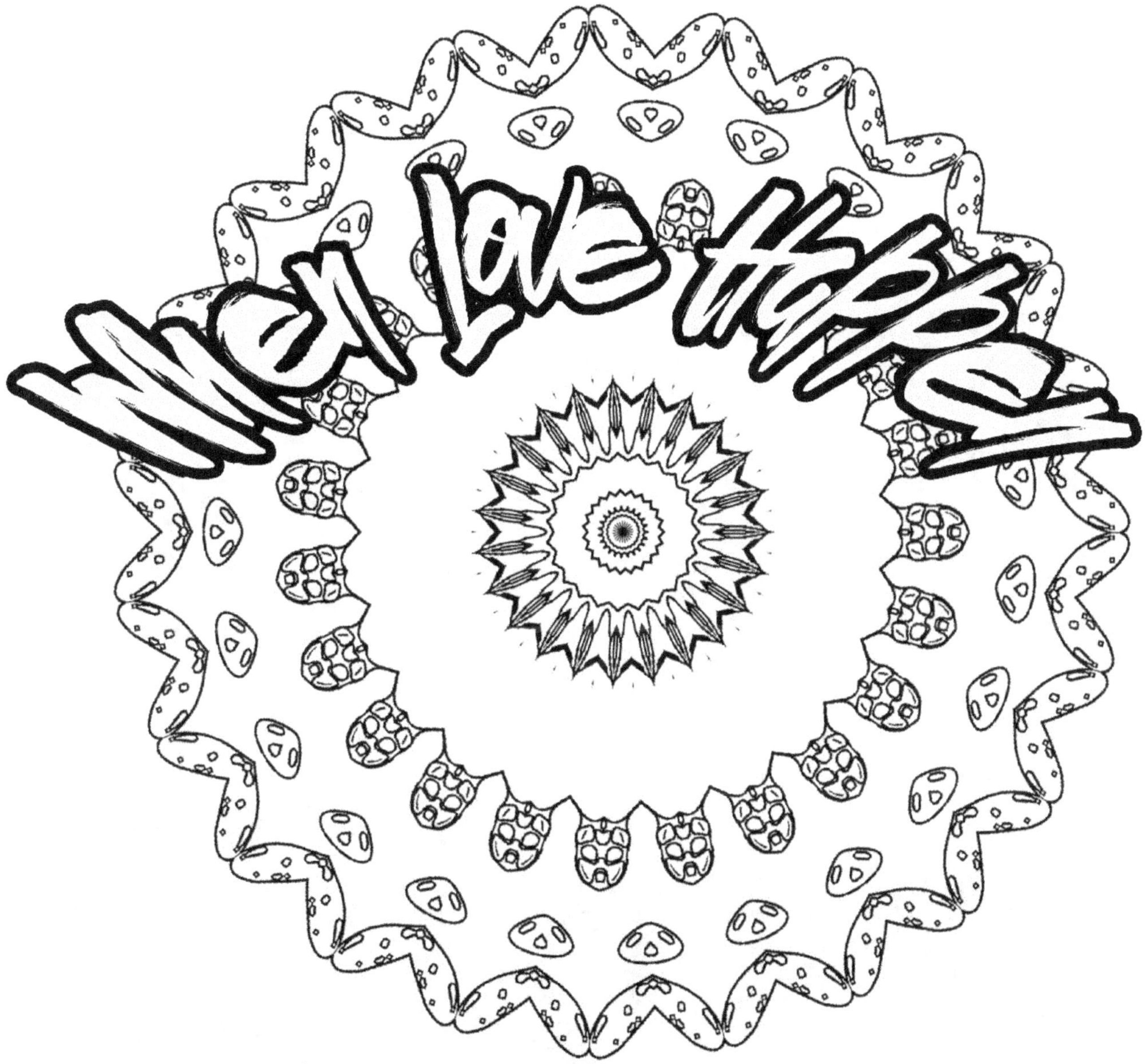
When Love Happens

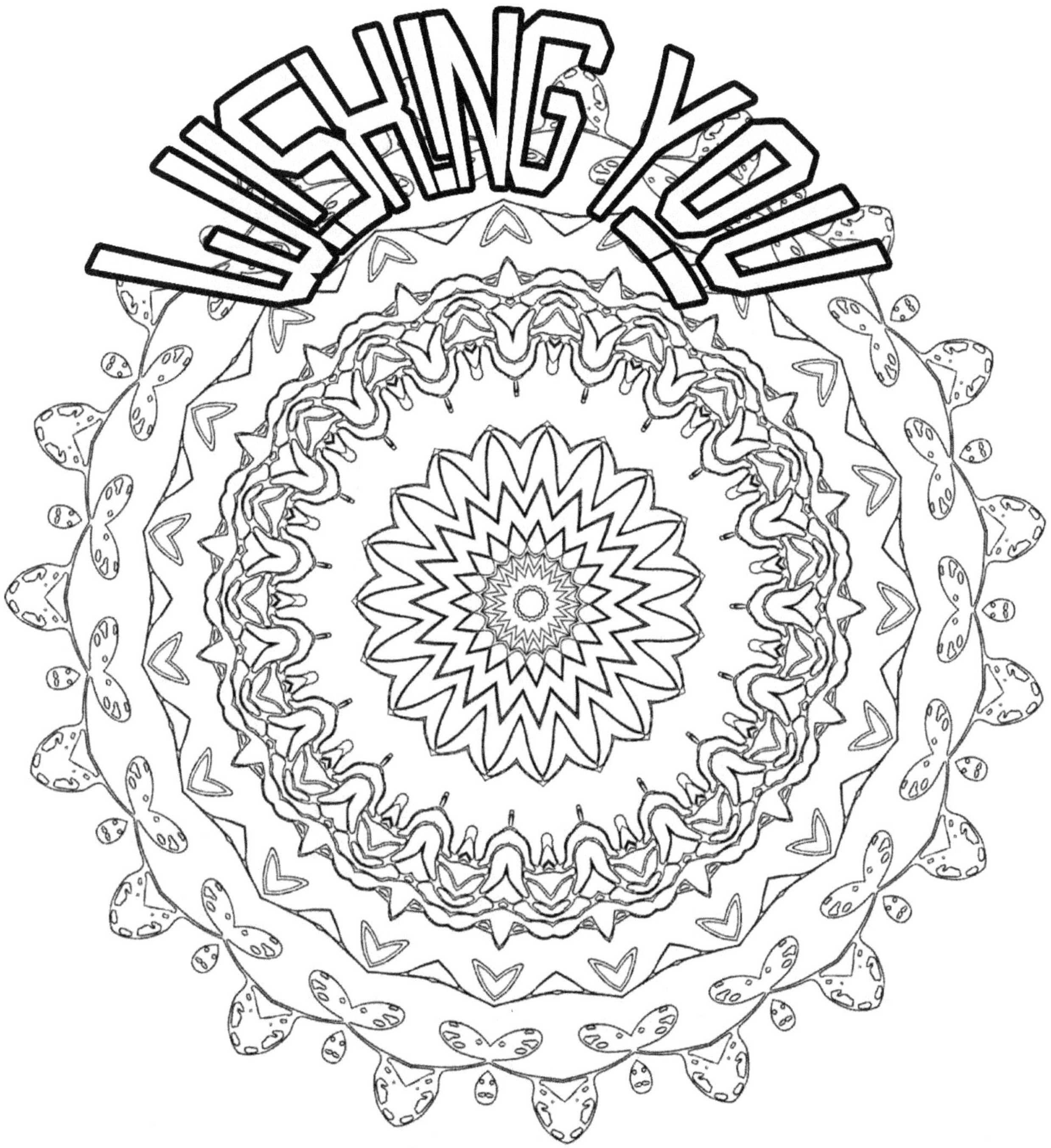
WISHING YOU

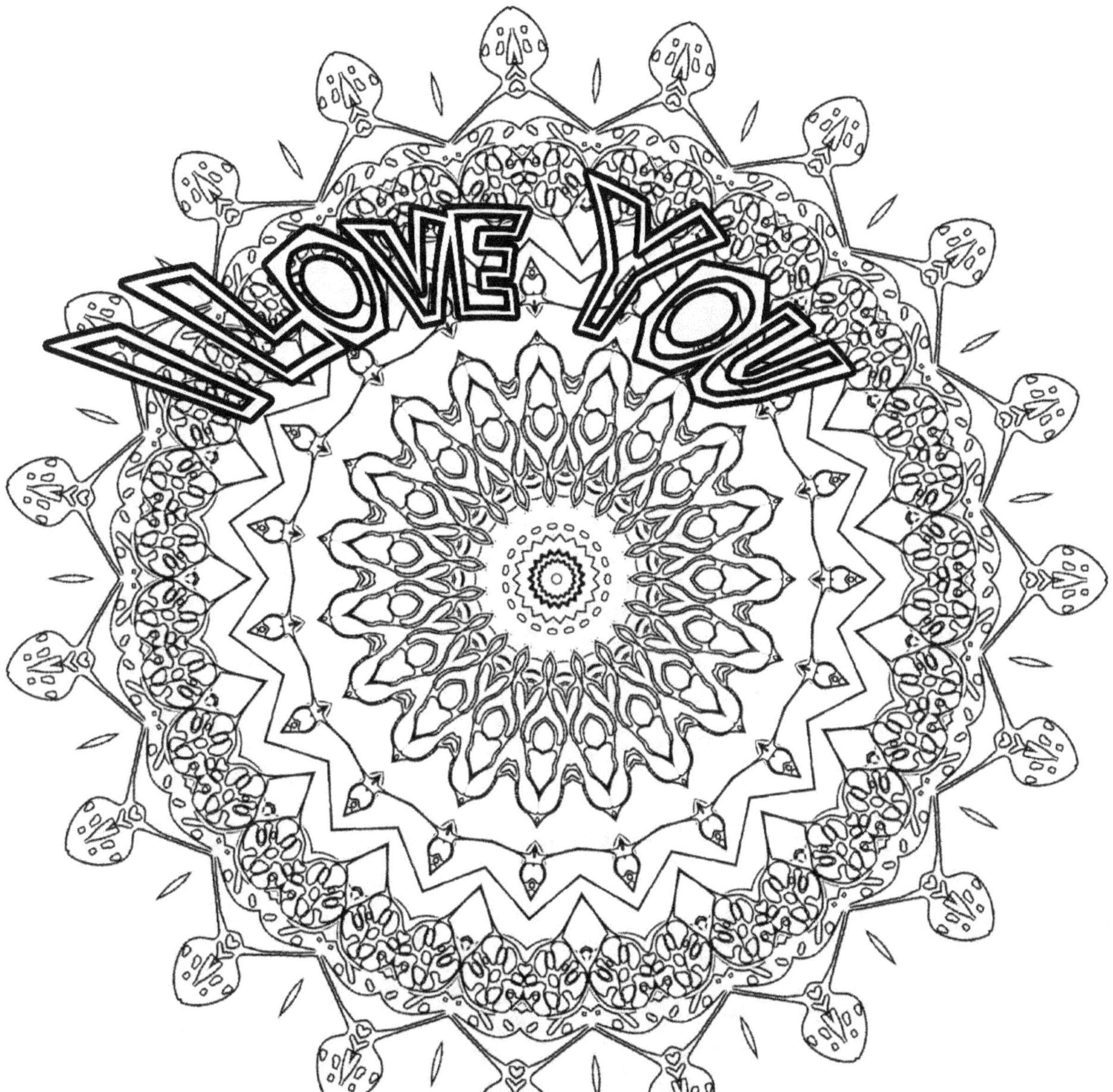
I LOVE YOU

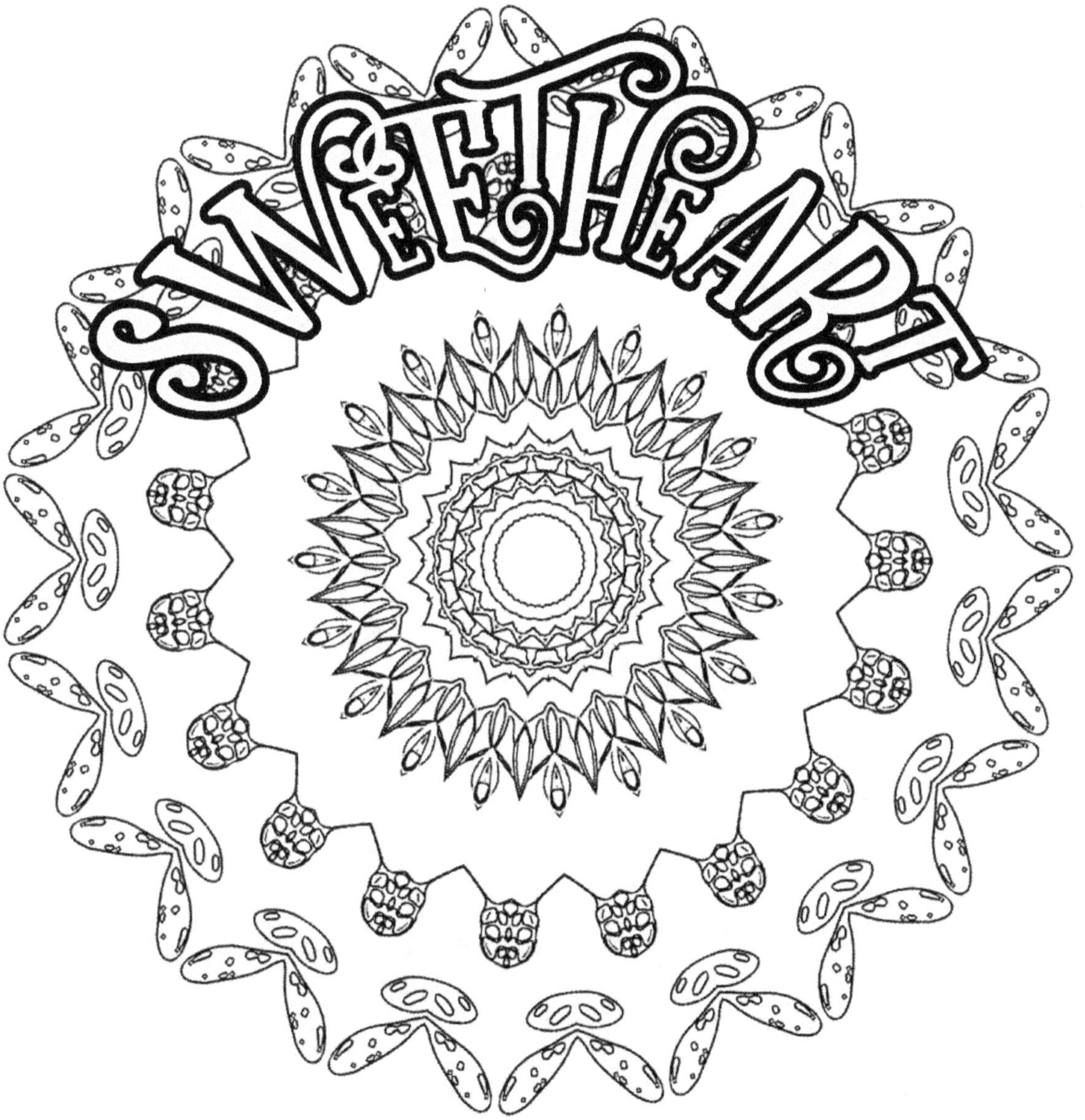
SWEETHEART

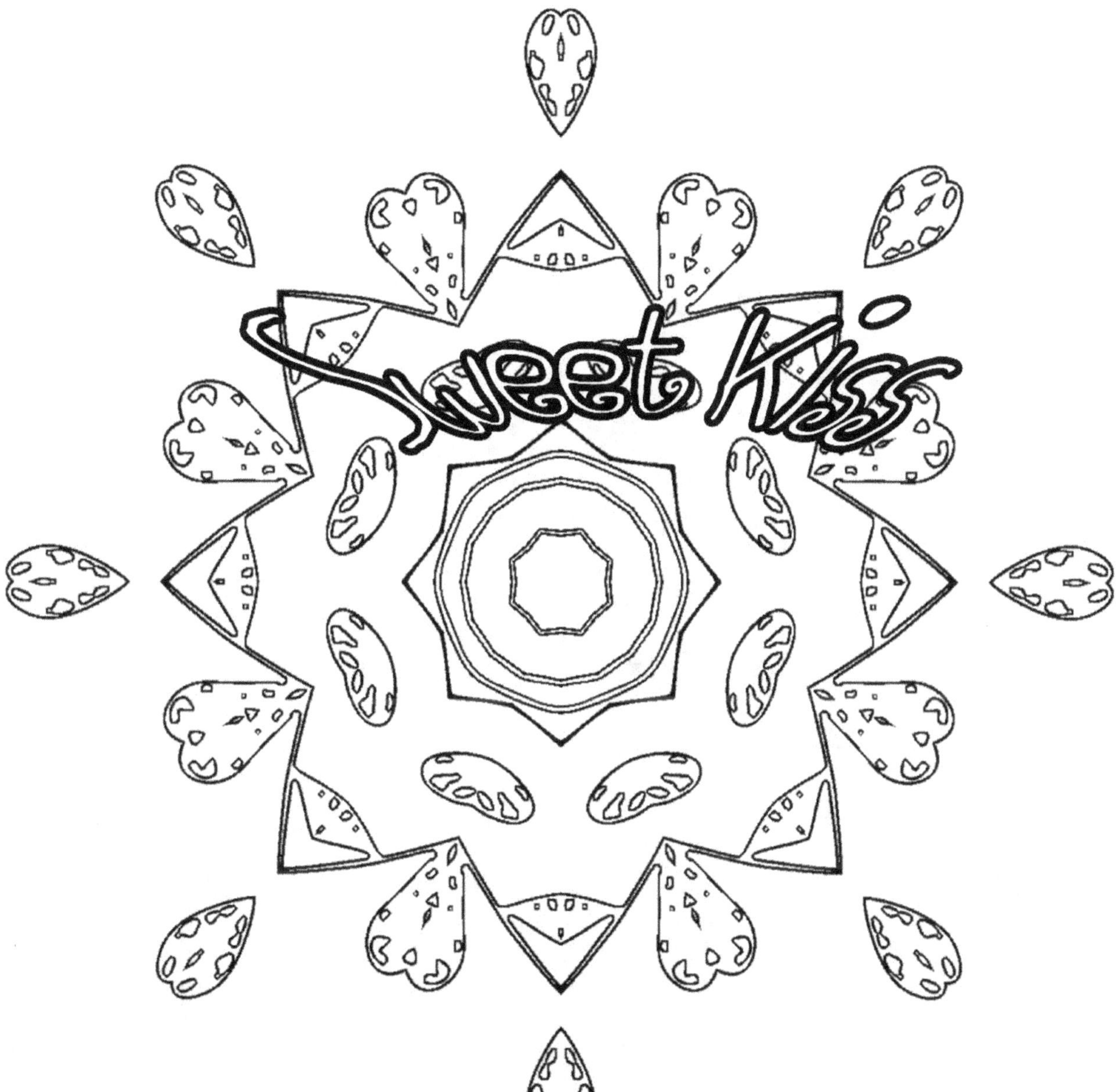
Sweet Kiss

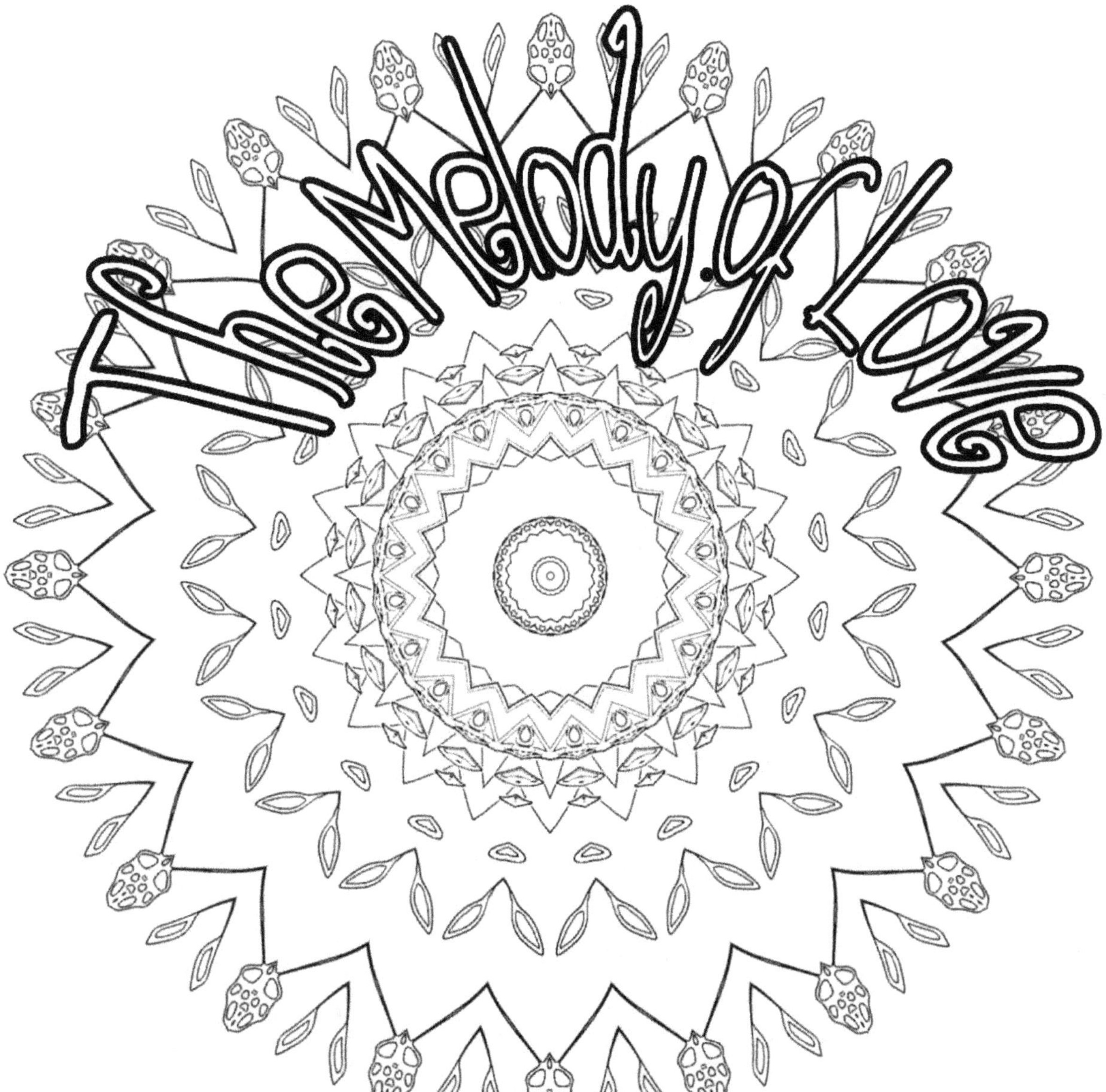
The Melody of Love

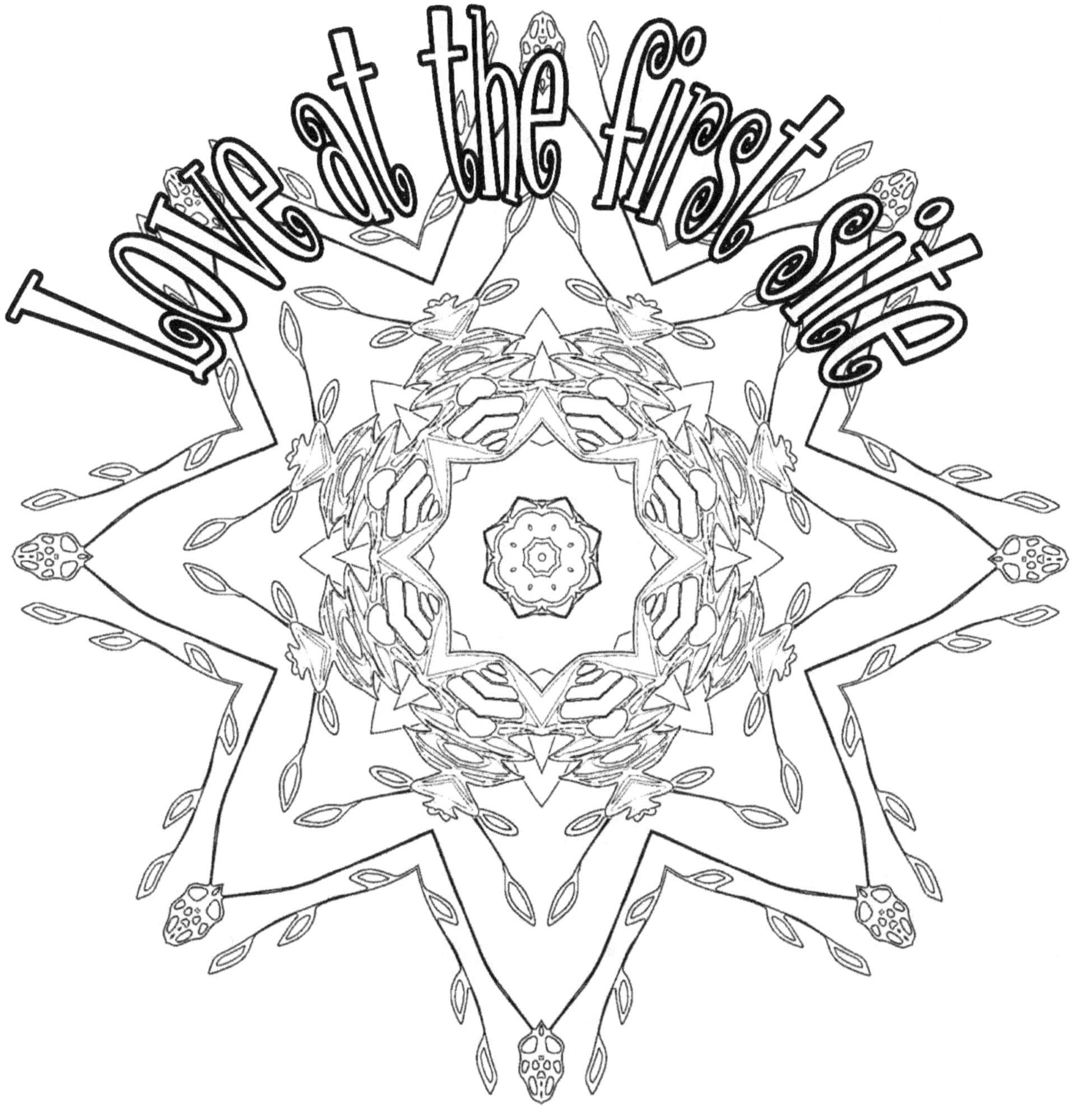
Love at the first site

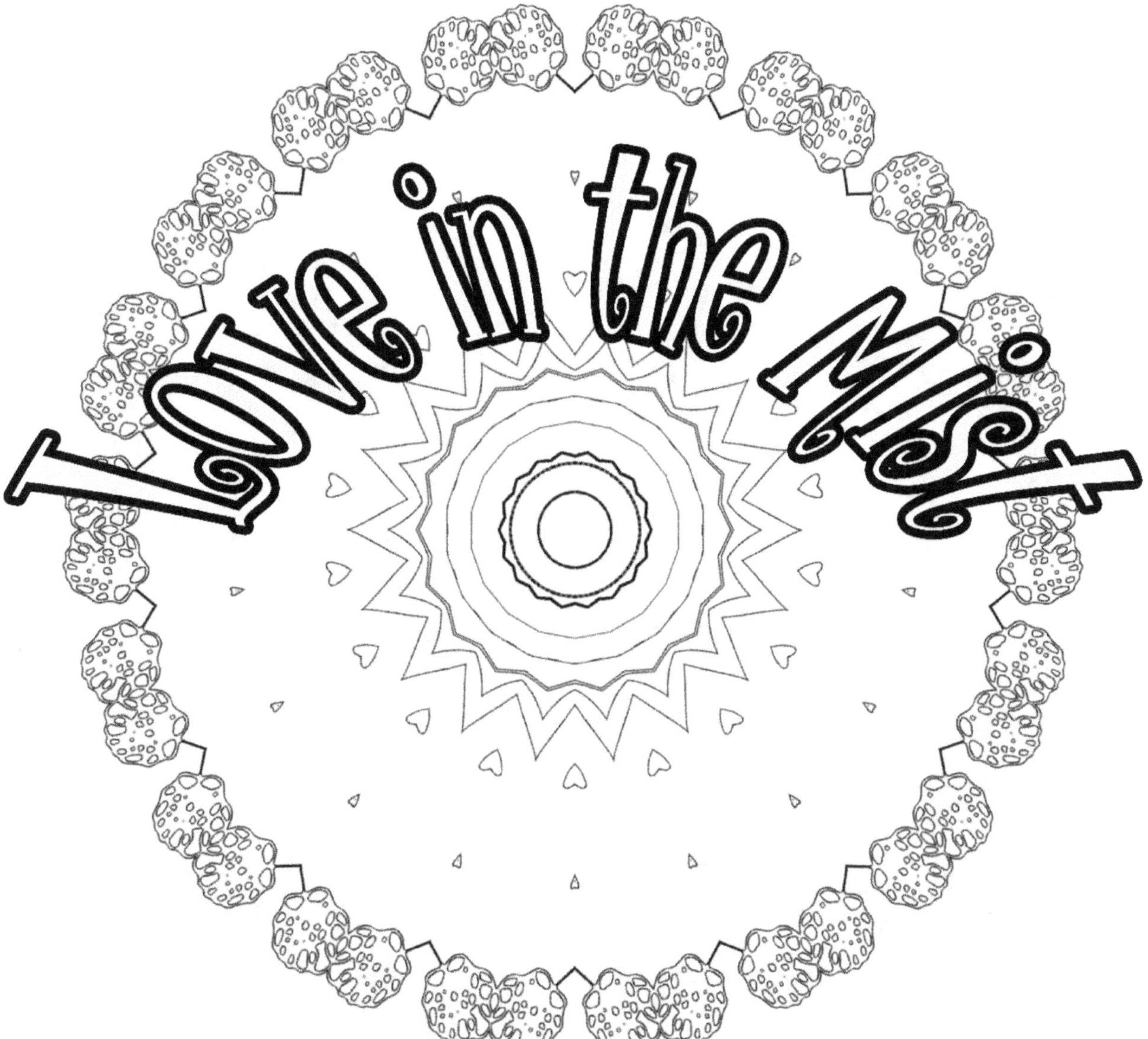
Love in the Mist

A Cup Of Love

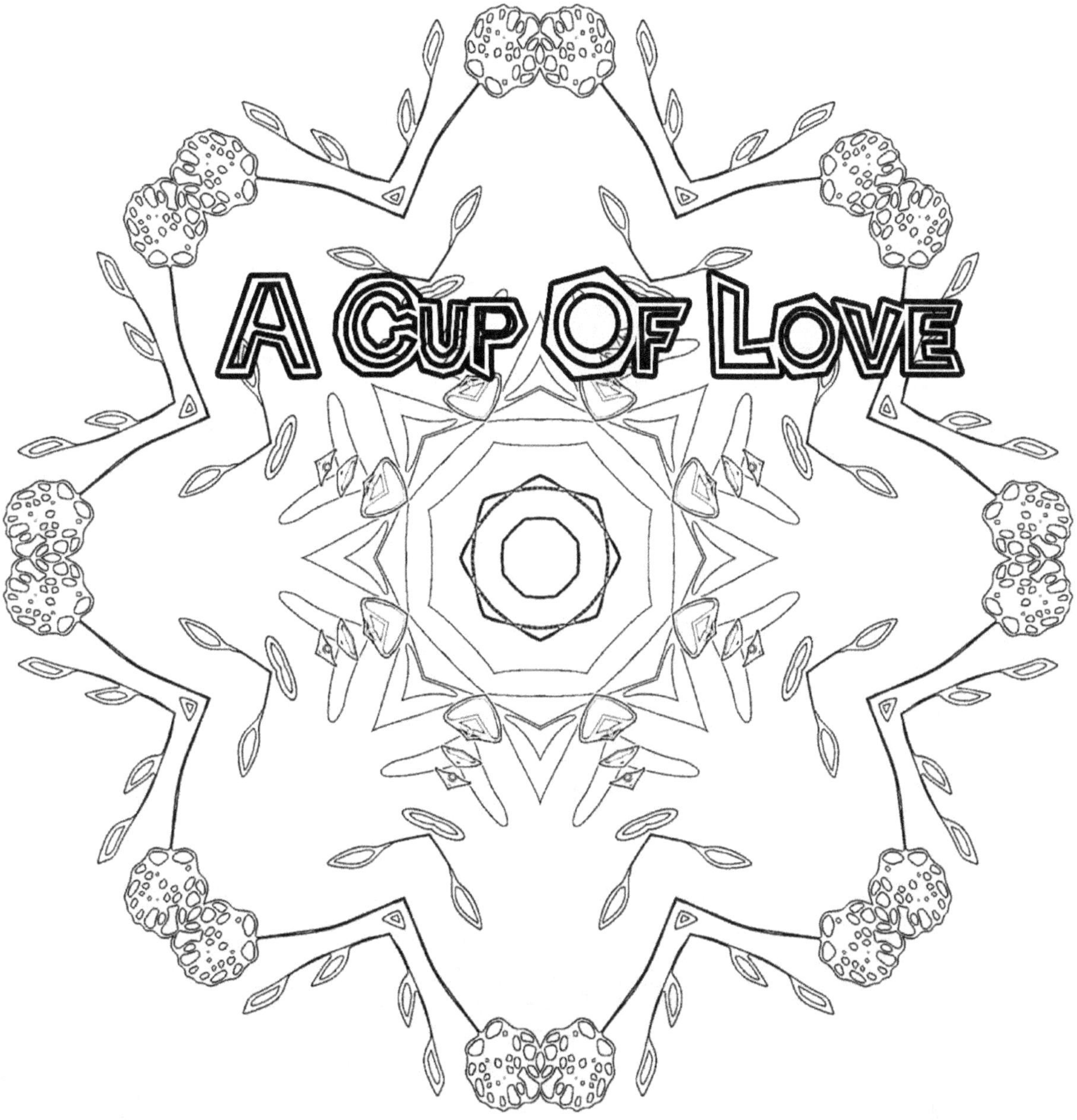

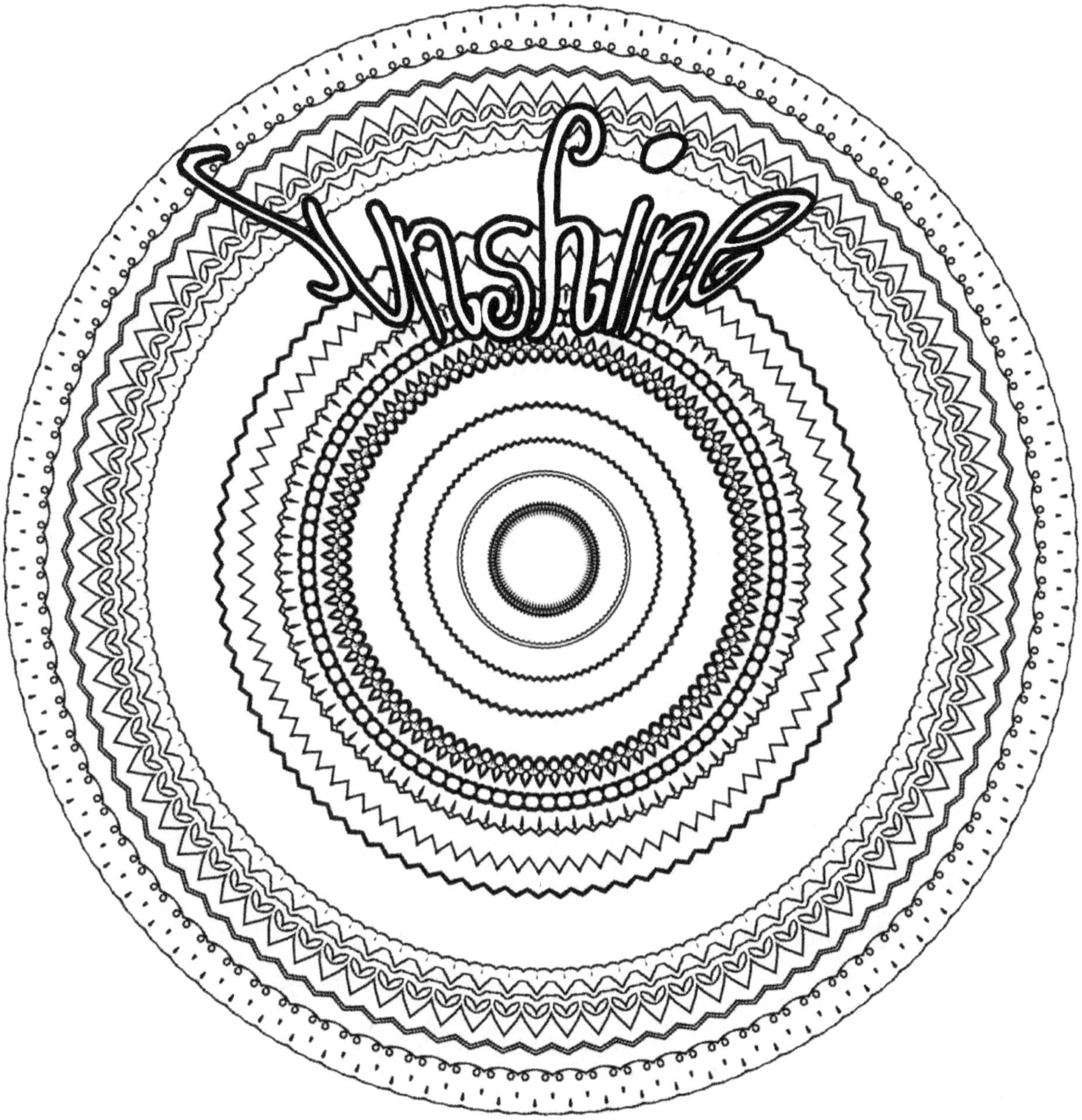
Sunshine

www.ingramcontent.com/pod-product-compliance
Lightning Source LLC
Chambersburg PA
CBHW081749170526
45167CB00009B/3980
9781543045208